CHRISTOPHER HART

Draw™

MANGA FANTASY

WATSON-GUPTILL
PUBLICATIONS/
NEW YORK

For Isabella
and Francesca

Senior Acquisitions Editor: Julie Mazur
Project Editor: Cathy Hennessy
Designer: Bob Fillie, Graphiti Design, Inc.
Production Manager: Hector Campbell
Text set in 12-pt. Frutiger Roman

First published in 2006 by
Watson-Guptill Publications,
a division of VNU Business Media, Inc.,
770 Broadway, New York, NY 10003
www.wgpub.com

Library of Congress Cataloging-in-Publication Data
Hart, Christopher.
    Kids draw Manga fantasy / Christopher Hart.
          p. cm. — (Kids draw)
Includes index.
ISBN 0-8230-2639-6
1. Comic books, strips, etc.—Japan—Technique—Juvenile literature.
2. Drawing—Technique—Juvenile literature.
3. Fantasy in art—Juvenile literature. I. Title.
    NC1764.5.J3H369275 2006
    741.5-dc22
                                                    2005025818

Printed in the United States of America

First printing, 2006

1 2 3 4 5 6 7 8 / 12 11 10 09 08 07 06 05

VISIT US AT

CONTENTS

INTRODUCTION

Manga is the Japanese style of comics that is sweeping the nation—and the world!

It's famous for big-eyed characters with delicate features and spiky hair. There are many different kinds of manga and one of the most popular is "fantasy manga."

The fantasy kingdom is filled with magical faeries, beautiful princesses, mermaids, wizards and warlocks, demon beasts, futuristic knights, and so much more. The stories about these supernatural beings are filled with magic, heroism, and mystery.

If you have ever wondered how to draw these enchanted beings this is the perfect book for you. Clear, step-by-step instructions make creating these fantasy characters simple and fun. You'll start off by learning how to draw the basic manga face and body, and then you'll quickly move on to super-cool stuff like creating magical effects, drawing different wings for enchanted beings, and designing your own fantasy costumes. Along the way, I will reveal some secret tips that will really make your drawings sparkle.

So get ready to let your imagination run wild as you enter the amazing world of fantasy manga!

MANGA FANTASY BASICS

Ready to have some fun? Let's start with the basics and then we'll build on your skills. Soon you'll be creating your own amazing fantasy characters!

Drawing Fantasy Boy Faces

The basic teen boy's face is soft, not angular—except for the chin, which is delicate and pointed. The eyes of fantasy boy characters are big, but not huge, as they are on some manga characters.

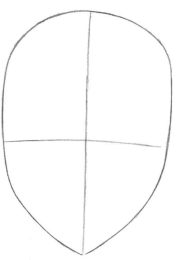

Draw light lines to guide you, then erase them at the end.

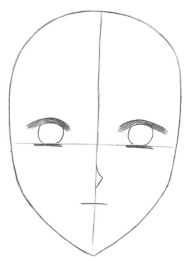

Make the upper eyelids thicker than the lower eyelids.

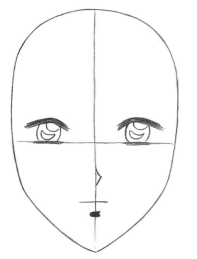

Add a small shadow under the lip.

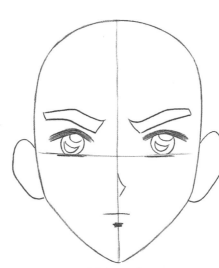

Draw thick eyebrows.

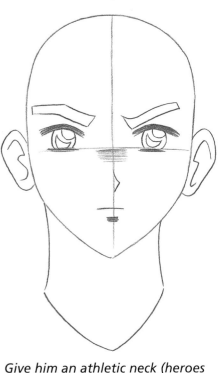

Give him an athletic neck (heroes never have skinny necks).

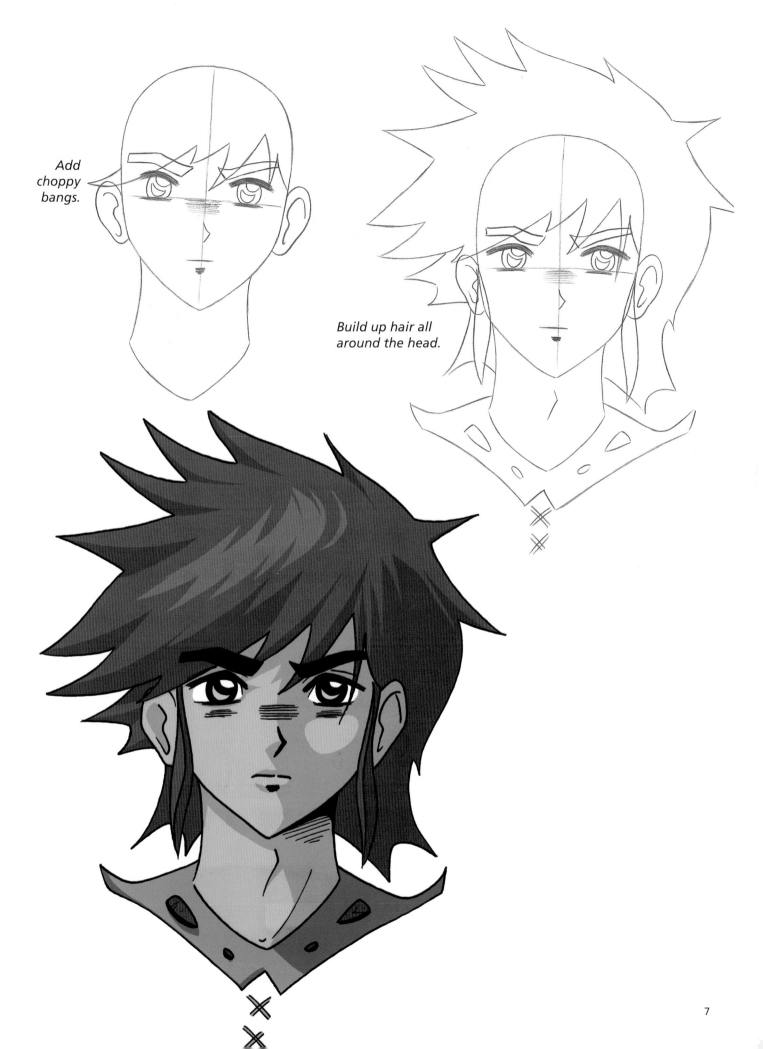

Add choppy bangs.

Build up hair all around the head.

Drawing Fantasy Girl Faces

The female face begins with the same soft shape as the male head but the jawline is a little fuller around the cheeks.

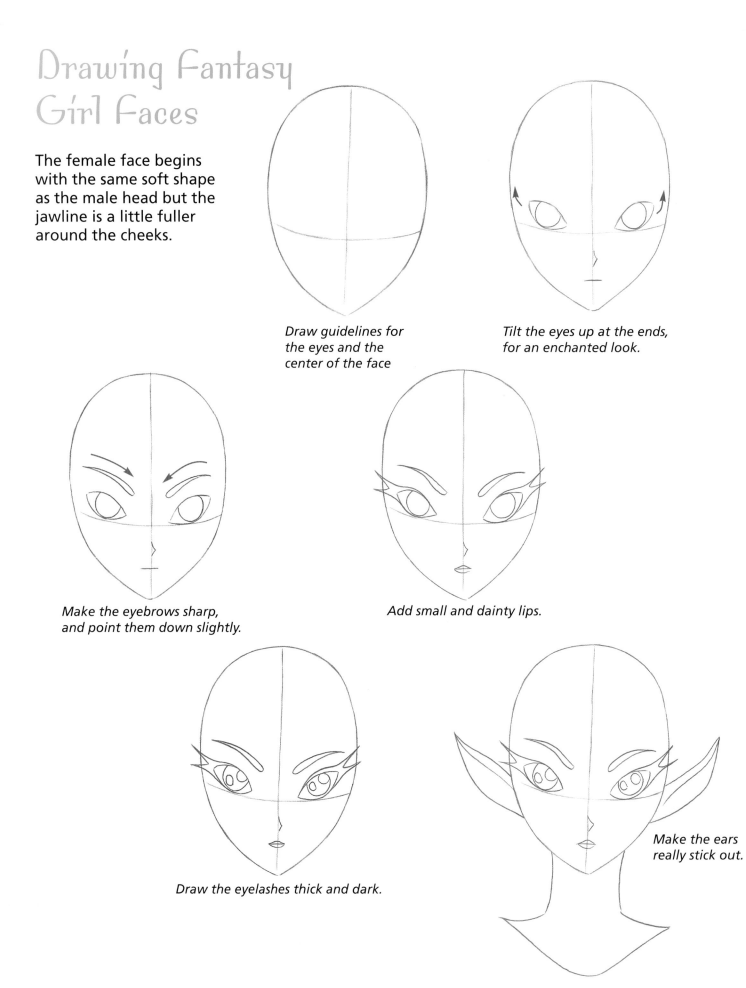

Draw guidelines for the eyes and the center of the face

Tilt the eyes up at the ends, for an enchanted look.

Make the eyebrows sharp, and point them down slightly.

Add small and dainty lips.

Draw the eyelashes thick and dark.

Make the ears really stick out.

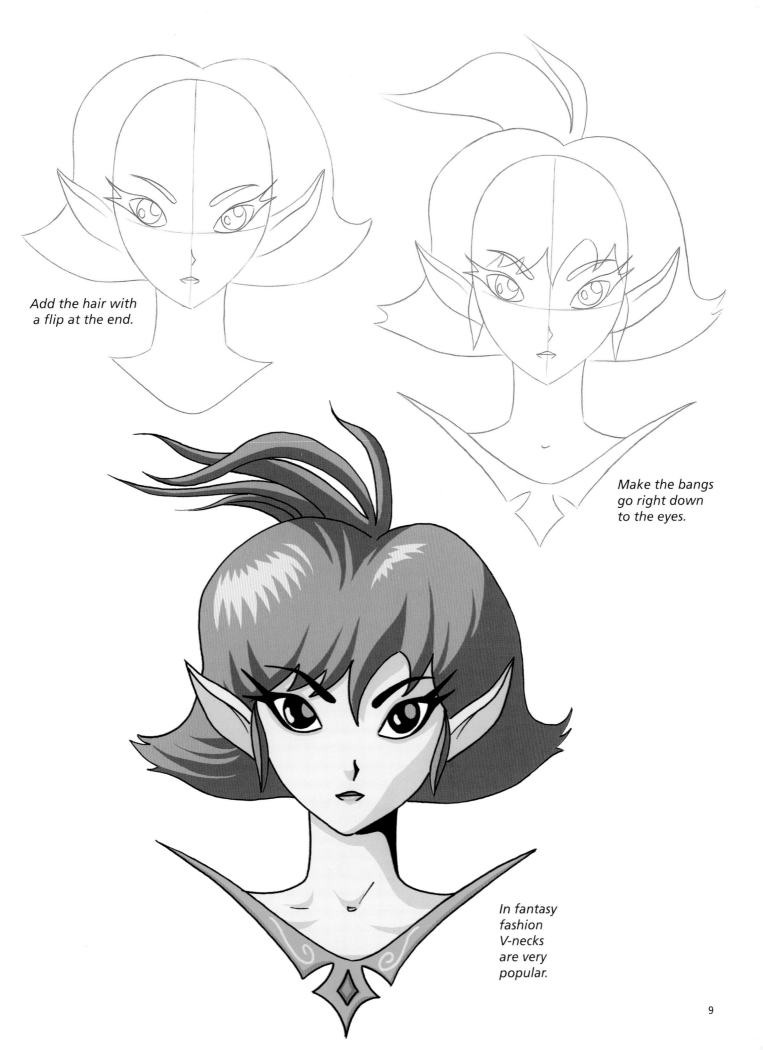

Add the hair with a flip at the end.

Make the bangs go right down to the eyes.

In fantasy fashion V-necks are very popular.

Designing Hair

It's fun to draw wild and stylish hairdos on your character. But the tricky part comes when you have to draw where the hairline meets the scalp. You need to know where the natural hairline falls on a character's head.

The "X" marks the center of the head, where a "middle part" would start. Manga characters always have big hair—it never lies flat.

CREATING SPIKY HAIR
Spiky hair is a classic feature of manga characters. The secret to drawing it is simple —make sure that all of the spikes travel in the same direction!

RIGHT
The spikes of the hair all travel in the same direction.

WRONG
The spikes of the hair travel in different directions.

Drawing the Power Fist

In fantasy manga the fist is the most dynamic hand pose. A character can raise it in anger, grip an object or a weapon with it, or use it to punch a bad guy's lights out! As you can see below, there are many angles from which we can draw the fist.

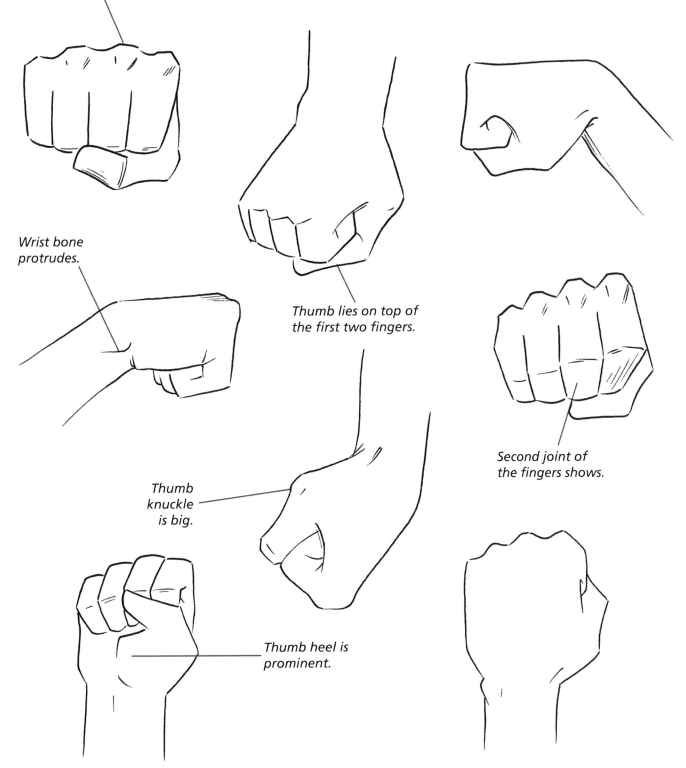

Each knuckle appears in the middle of the finger.

Wrist bone protrudes.

Thumb lies on top of the first two fingers.

Thumb knuckle is big.

Second joint of the fingers shows.

Thumb heel is prominent.

Drawing Spectacular Eyes

Manga characters are famous for their sparkling eyes with giant "shines" inside them—the shine is light reflecting off the dark parts of the eye. The trick is to create patterns and designs within the eye, and not just a plain circle for a shine. Check out these examples, and then try drawing your own.

FEMALE EYE—SIDE VIEW
Note that her long lashes appear not only in front of the eye, but behind the eye as well.

MALE EYE—SIDE VIEW

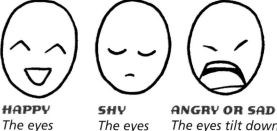

CLOSED EYES
There are three basic expressions caused by closed eyes:

HAPPY
The eyes curve down.

SHY
The eyes curve up.

ANGRY OR SAD
The eyes tilt down, toward the nose.

Beginners often draw the neck straight up and down. This is a mistake—but one that now you'll be able to avoid. Draw the neck at an angle instead. It'll look much more natural.

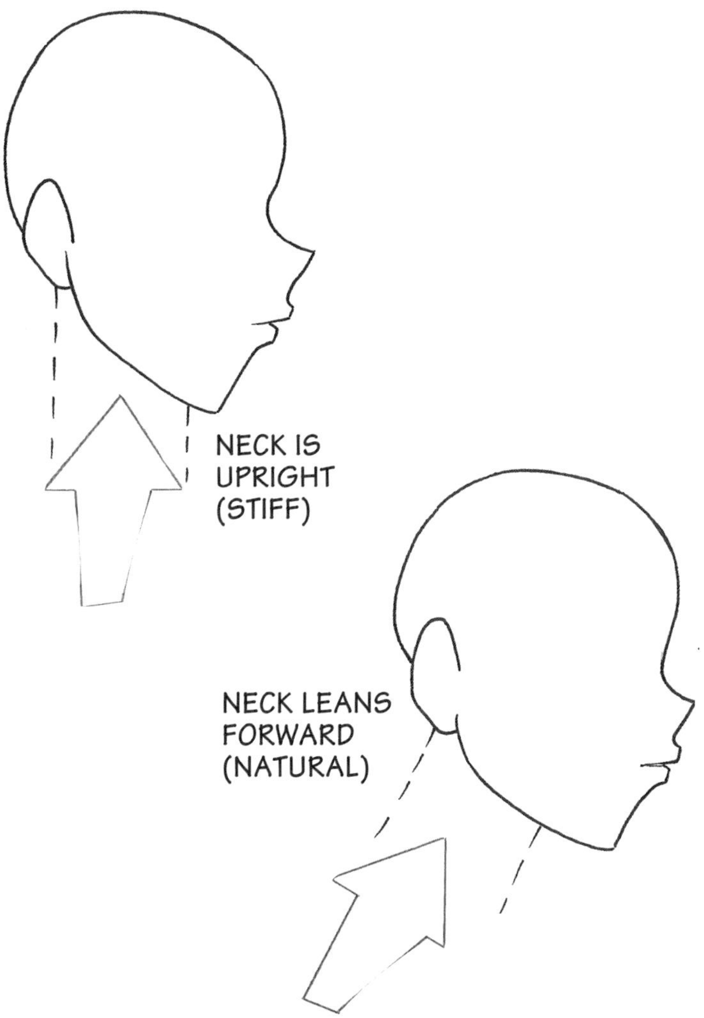

NECK IS
UPRIGHT
(STIFF)

NECK LEANS
FORWARD
(NATURAL)

Drawing the Male Body

When drawing the body, there are some simple, but little known, tricks you can use to make sure your proportions are correct. Take a look at the labels, and you'll see that it's easy!

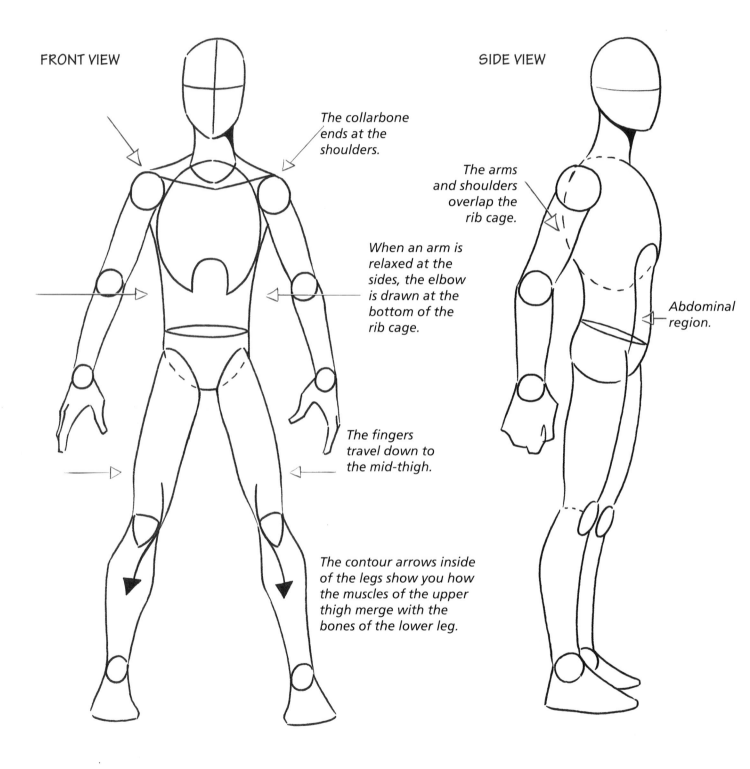

FRONT VIEW

SIDE VIEW

The collarbone ends at the shoulders.

When an arm is relaxed at the sides, the elbow is drawn at the bottom of the rib cage.

The fingers travel down to the mid-thigh.

The contour arrows inside of the legs show you how the muscles of the upper thigh merge with the bones of the lower leg.

The arms and shoulders overlap the rib cage.

Abdominal region.

Many beginners draw the body with straight lines—but this is a mistake. The body is dynamic. It has lots of curves, even on limbs that have fairly straight bones.

BODY DRAWN WITH STRAIGHT LINES (WRONG)
Straight lines make the body look stiff and awkward.

BODY DRAWN WITH CURVED LINES (RIGHT)
Curved lines make the body look natural and lifelike.

Drawing the Female Body

The female figure can be challenging to draw. But it's much easier if we simply divide the torso into three parts: chest, midsection, and hips. Note that the shoulders and hips are equally wide, giving the female figure an "hourglass" look.

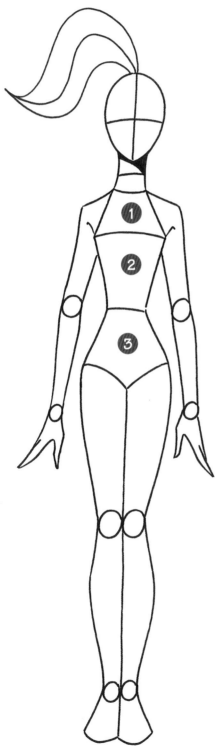

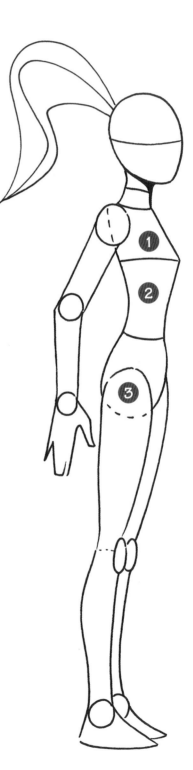

The secret to making a pose look natural is simple: put more of the weight on one leg than the other. Many beginning artists draw their characters with equal weight on both legs. But who stands like that, other than soldiers in the army? No one.

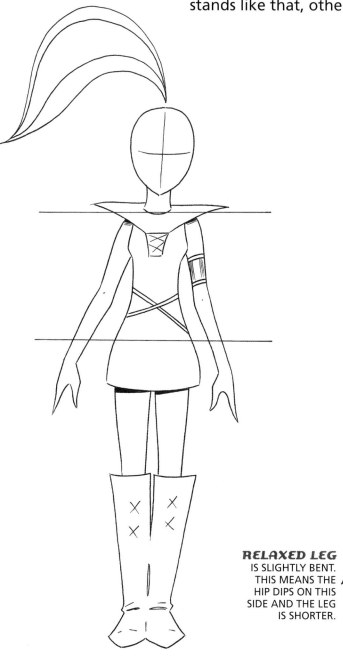

RELAXED LEG IS SLIGHTLY BENT. THIS MEANS THE HIP DIPS ON THIS SIDE AND THE LEG IS SHORTER.

WEIGHT-BEARING LEG IS STRAIGHT. THIS PUSHES THE HIP UP ON THIS SIDE AND MAKES THIS LEG LONGER.

EQUAL WEIGHT PLACED ON BOTH LEGS
Both legs have equal weight on them. That means that the shoulders and hips are straight, parallel to the floor. See how stiff the pose looks?

NATURAL-LOOKING POSE
The leg that is directly underneath the body bears most of the weight. The relaxed leg moves away from the body, with the knee slightly bent. This causes the shoulders and the hips to tilt at opposing angles.

FAERIES AND KNIGHTS

Now that you know the basics, it's time to create your very own fantasy characters!

Faerie Princess

Princesses are always charming and captivating. When you see one, you know something magical and wondrous is in the air. We'll start with a "medium shot," which means from the waist up. The medium shot is very effective, because we can get the full feeling of the character without the complexity of drawing the entire figure.

Natural curve of spine

Dip chin down into shoulder for a mysterious look.

DRAWING THE FAERIE EYE

The eye of the faerie is different from that of other manga characters. It tilts up at the ends, even more than on a regular female character. The eye is also narrower, and the eyelashes, as well as the eyebrow, are sharper. The eyeball itself is tucked deeper into the upper eyelid, adding a mysterious touch.

REGULAR FEMALE EYE
The regular female eye has a bigger eyeball.

FAERIE EYE
Note the deep tilt of the faerie eye, and how the upper eyelid rests heavily upon it.

Magical jewels and crystals are a popular part of the manga fantasy genre. These jewels bestow special powers upon the holder, and are therefore sought by many—especially those with evil aspirations.

Faerie Sorcerer

Is he good or evil? That's for you to decide, for he is a powerful being who uses magic for his own purposes. Give him a sleek face and pointy chin. And if you want to make him look extra-sinister (which I do!), give him tiny eyebrows and a long, slim nose.

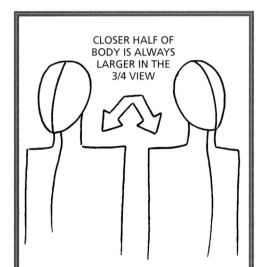

CLOSER HALF OF BODY IS ALWAYS LARGER IN THE 3/4 VIEW

SIDE HINT
This character is in a 3/4 view. That means he's not facing directly at us (which would be a "front view"), and he's not facing sideways (which would be a "profile"). Instead, he is halfway between the two. When drawing a character in a 3/4 view, divide him in half, from top to bottom, with a "center line." Make sure that the half of the body that is closest to you is larger than the half of the body that is furthest away from you.

High collars are popular for fantasy characters.

The first "knuckle" of the thumb appears at the base of the hand, and sticks out.

Standing Faerie

Drawing a faerie standing in a sweeping breeze makes her look very appealing. Remember to first sketch the torso by dividing it into three parts, then draw her body with lots of curving lines. And to make the pose more dramatic, try combining two different angles: draw her body turned at a 3/4 angle, but have her head face us at a front angle.

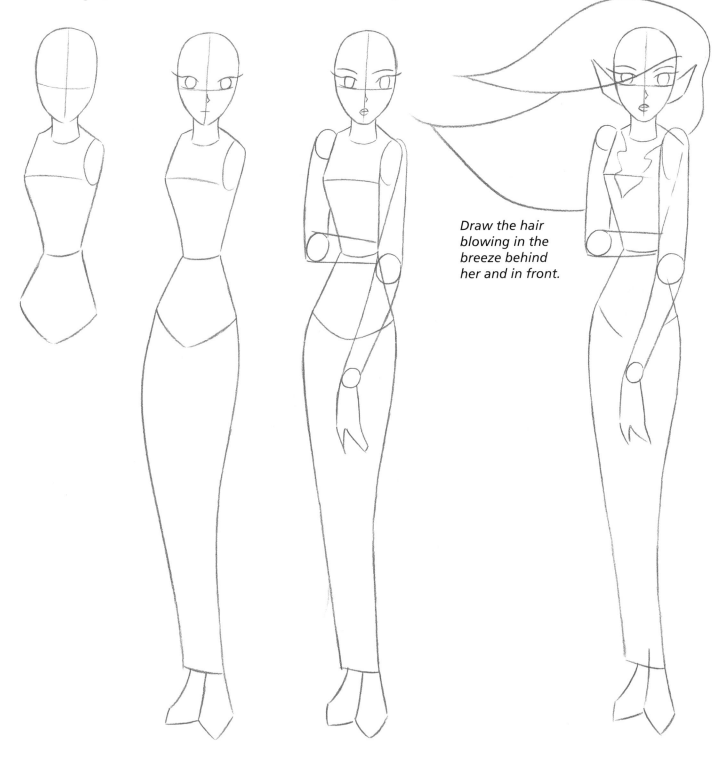

Draw the hair blowing in the breeze behind her and in front.

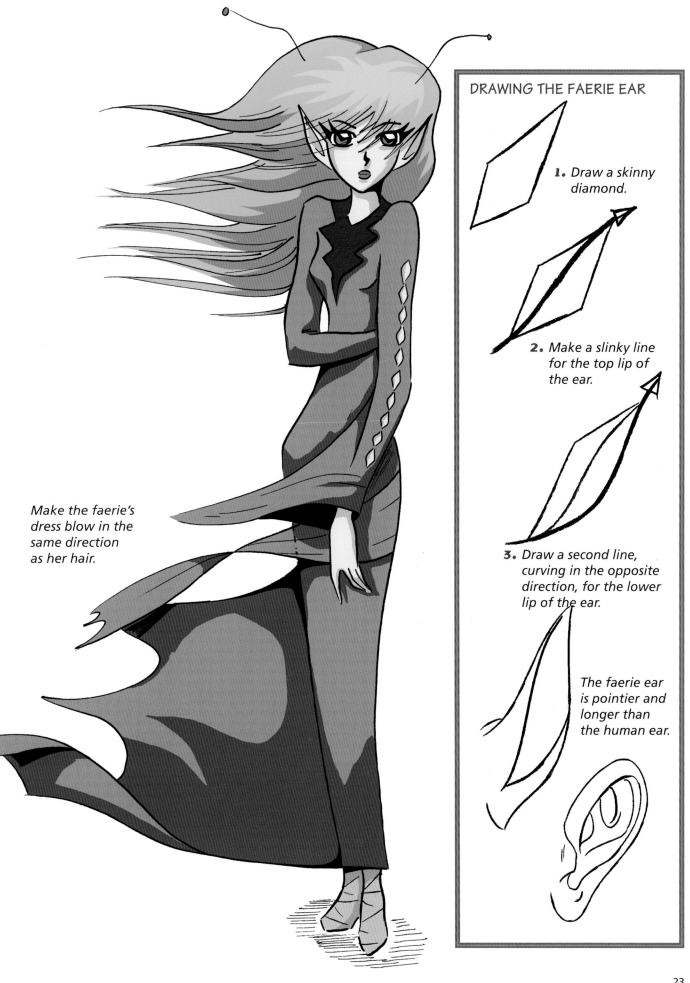

Make the faerie's dress blow in the same direction as her hair.

DRAWING THE FAERIE EAR

1. Draw a skinny diamond.

2. Make a slinky line for the top lip of the ear.

3. Draw a second line, curving in the opposite direction, for the lower lip of the ear.

The faerie ear is pointier and longer than the human ear.

Faerie and Baby

Faeries are attentive mothers and always keep their children close to them. They need to protect them from the many dangers that lurk in the forest. Charmed creatures, predatory animals, and evil spirits abound. But through it all, the magic of the faerie world keeps shining.

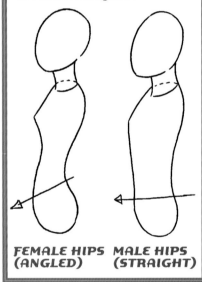

MALE VERSUS FEMALE HIPS
Female hips slant forward, at an angle, while male hips are much straighter.

FEMALE HIPS (ANGLED)   **MALE HIPS (STRAIGHT)**

The back has a feminine, sweeping curve to it.

The line of the backpack doubles as the line of her upper arm!

The tummy sticks out just a touch, caused by the hips slanting forward.

Two small hands are all that's needed for a baby faeirie—the arms don't show at this angle.

Fantasy Knight

Knights are especially popular in fantasy-based manga. They are often portrayed with special powers and possess fantasy weapons. But no matter how you design your fantasy character, it all begins with the basic knight costume.

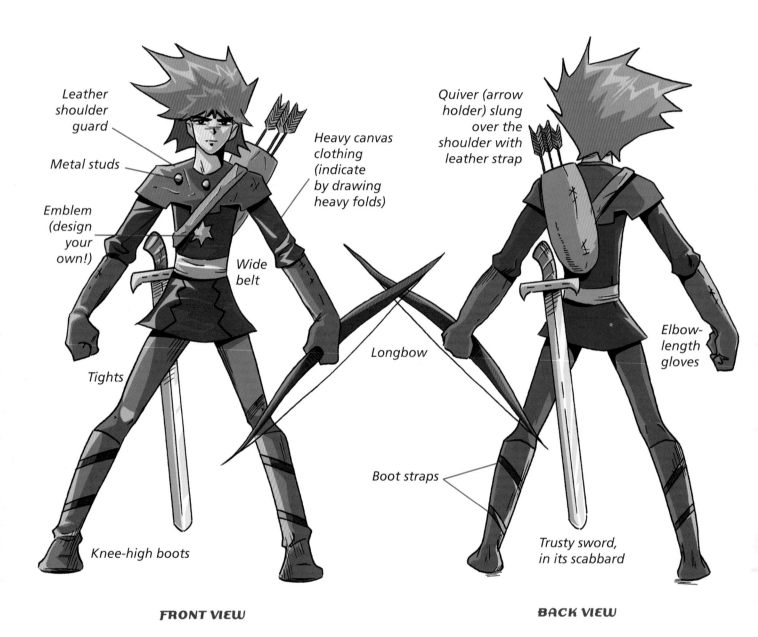

Leather shoulder guard

Metal studs

Emblem (design your own!)

Tights

Knee-high boots

Heavy canvas clothing (indicate by drawing heavy folds)

Wide belt

Longbow

Quiver (arrow holder) slung over the shoulder with leather strap

Elbow-length gloves

Boot straps

Trusty sword, in its scabbard

FRONT VIEW

BACK VIEW

Heroic Knight

Sword in hand, the heroic knight is ready to defend good against evil. His torch lights the way as he bravely enters the dangerous caves in the mountains of the green dragons.

Make the cuffs of the gloves oval.

HOW TO "DRAW THROUGH" AN OBJECT

Imagine an islander is holding a decorative pole in his hand. "Drawing through" the object means that we sketch the entire pole, even the part that will be hidden by his hand. In this way, we will be able to keep the pole straight.

POLE IS "DRAWN THROUGH" HAND

POLE IS "DRAWN THROUGH" DECORATION

CORRECT
By drawing through the hand, we make sure the pole is straight.

POLE IS NOT "DRAWN THROUGH" DECORATION

POLE IS NOT "DRAWN THROUGH" HAND

INCORRECT
When we don't draw through the hand, the result is the pole is not straight.

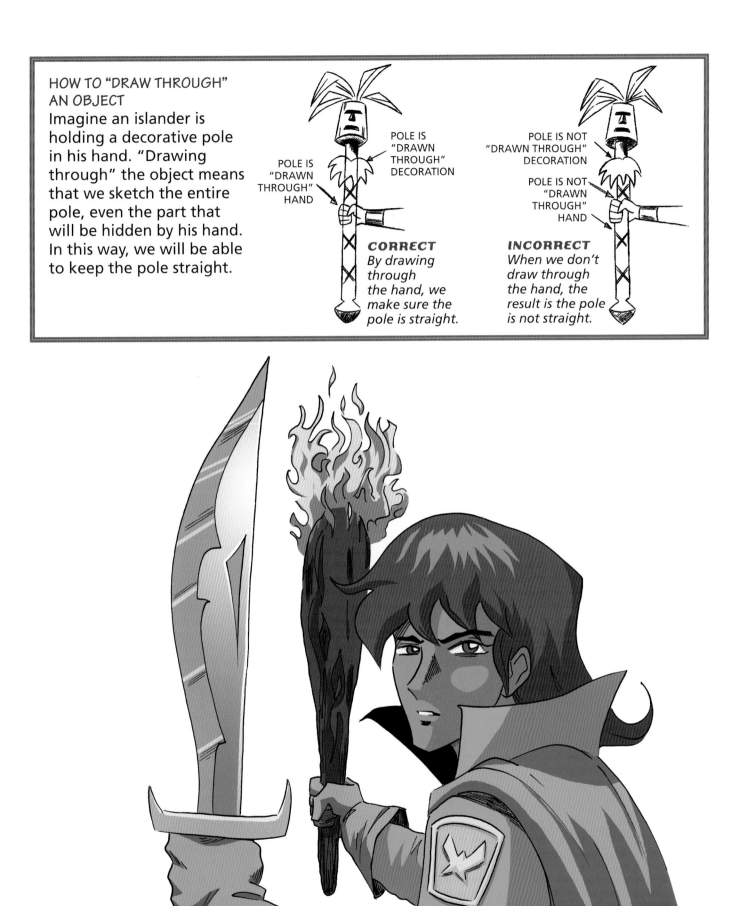

Knights and Castles

Backgrounds can really liven up a scene. They ground it in time and place. Many beginning artists draw the characters on one spot on the page and the background objects on another. That's good in theory. But in practice, it's not so good. It usually leaves an empty space between the character and the background object. The trick is to have the characters OVERLAP the background. That makes the character one with the scene and creates a feeling of depth.

The far shoulder peeks out from behind the chest.

FLYING CHARACTERS

Winged beings are really popular in fantasy manga. They can be male or female and take the form of anything from angels to magical guardians to warriors.

Drawing Wings

The most common type of wing is the feathered wing. Many beginners know how to draw a simple wing. But very few know the trick to creating fantasy wings. So stay tuned while I open up the vault and pull out another secret technique.

ONLY OKAY
The bottom, feathered part slants inward, toward the body. Not a great look.

BETTER
By slanting the feathered part outward, you create a more graceful look.

BEST!
Turn the tops of the wings inward and you'll have a slick, awesome look for your fantasy character.

Advanced Fantasy-Wing Workshop

In addition to the feathered wing, there are four other types of fantasy wings. Each one conveys a different feeling, so you can use them to show the personality of your fantasy character.

DRAGON WINGS
Evil beings have these types of wings. They have claws at the top and are a combination of pterodactyl and bat wings.

BUTTERFLY WINGS
These wings are for beautiful faeries.

DRAGONFLY WINGS
Also for faeries from the forests and woods, these are often drawn as double wings on each side.

RUFFLED FEATHER WINGS
A more detailed version of regular feather wings. They make a character more elegant and may be used for male or female fantasy characters.

Fantasy Guardian

The fantasy guardian is a serene being, but when called to action he can instantly transform into a fearless fighter. He usually dresses in a fantasy prince outfit and has long, flowing hair.

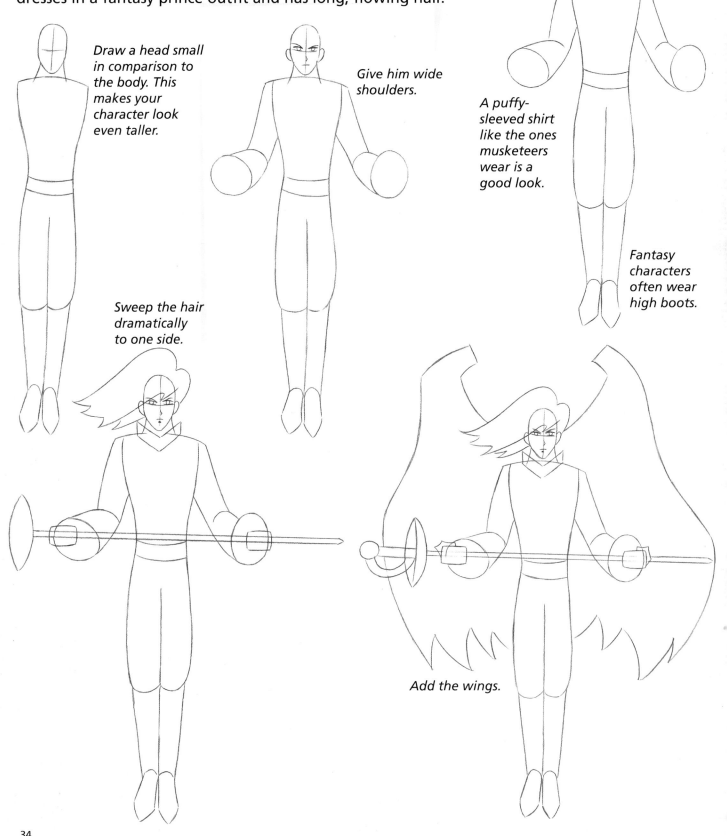

Draw a head small in comparison to the body. This makes your character look even taller.

Give him wide shoulders.

A puffy-sleeved shirt like the ones musketeers wear is a good look.

Fantasy characters often wear high boots.

Sweep the hair dramatically to one side.

Add the wings.

Winged Fantasy Angel

Fantasy angels are always tranquil and beautiful. This charming pose shows one sitting on her knees, facing forward.

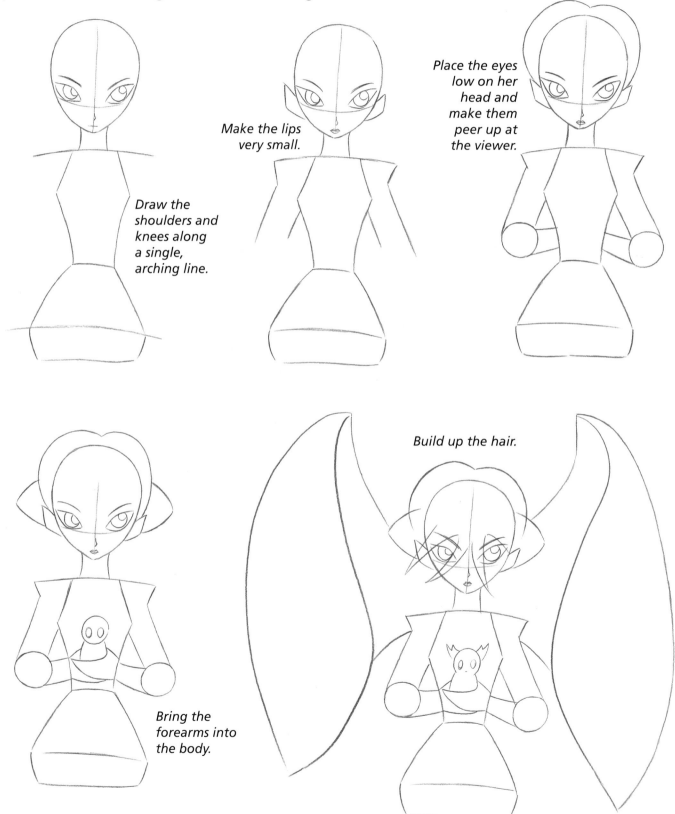

Draw the shoulders and knees along a single, arching line.

Make the lips very small.

Place the eyes low on her head and make them peer up at the viewer.

Bring the forearms into the body.

Build up the hair.

Faeries in Flight

Faeires are light, nimble beings. They can be found hovering over a flower, or sometimes above a group of lost hikers, offering to guide them to safety. But when threatened, faeries dash and dart with the quickness of a hummingbird. Therefore, their flying poses must be athletic and streamlined.

The arms are straight, making her pose more streamlined.

Note the gently curving line of the leg.

The skirt trails off, indicating motion.

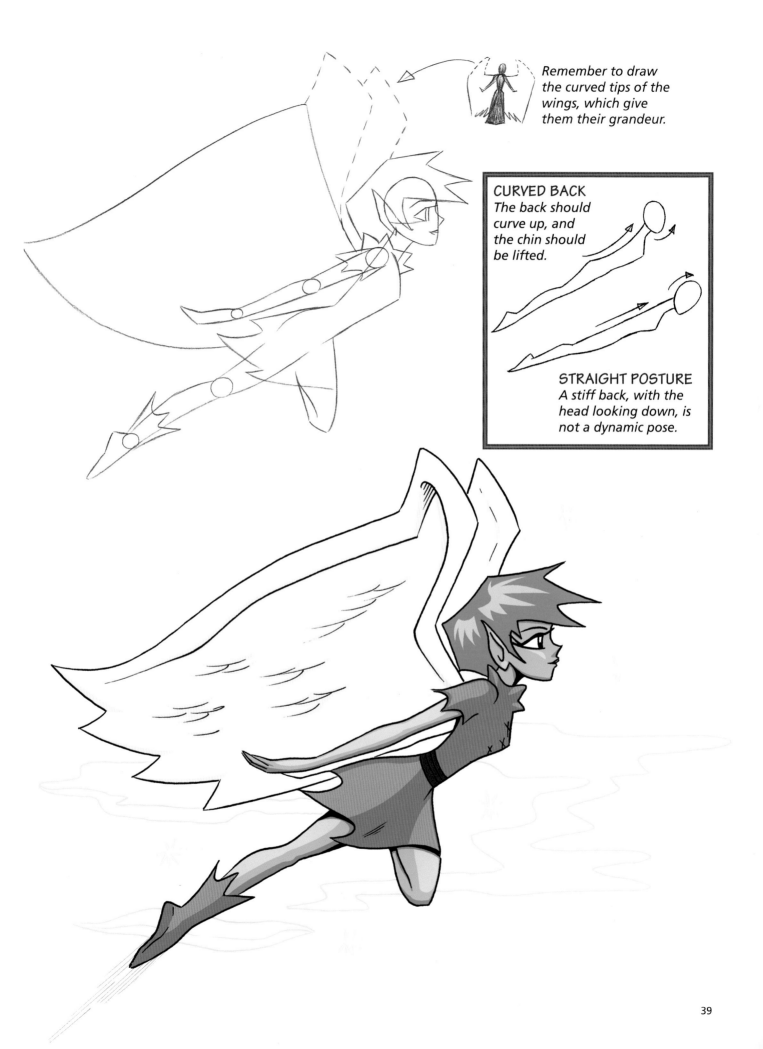

Remember to draw the curved tips of the wings, which give them their grandeur.

CURVED BACK
The back should curve up, and the chin should be lifted.

STRAIGHT POSTURE
A stiff back, with the head looking down, is not a dynamic pose.

MAGICAL EFFECTS!

Magical effects add excitement to a scene, and are an important part of the fantasy style. It's really cool to draw lightning bolts and other special effects, but first make sure that your character is well drawn.

See how the front leg looks longer than the back leg, even though we know they are really the same size? The front arm also looks longer than the back one. This is because of *perspective*, an important principle in drawing that says things closer to you will look larger than things that are farther away.

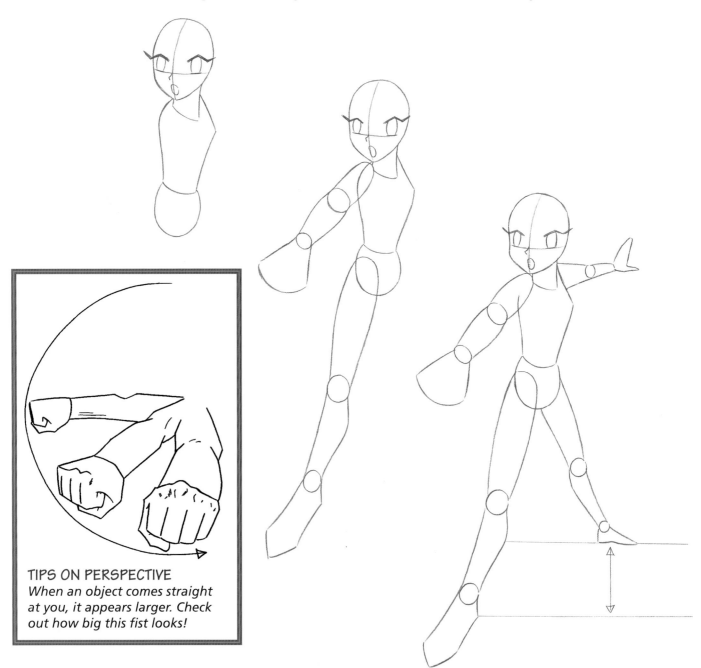

TIPS ON PERSPECTIVE
When an object comes straight at you, it appears larger. Check out how big this fist looks!

Give your character a magical weapon with special powers.

Jewels are always popular on wands.

MAGICAL ENERGY FIELD
A magical energy field surrounds a crystal or a jewel without actually touching it. Although the energy field is curved, I like to add some sharp edges to make it look more dramatic. Secondary special effects like sparks, stars, and spirals are always fun to add.

Creating Threads of Magic

This enchanted character has the power to conjure magic out of thin air. She can weave together a tapestry of magical forces and use them to cast a spell on an enemy, or call on great forces to assist her when she is in danger.

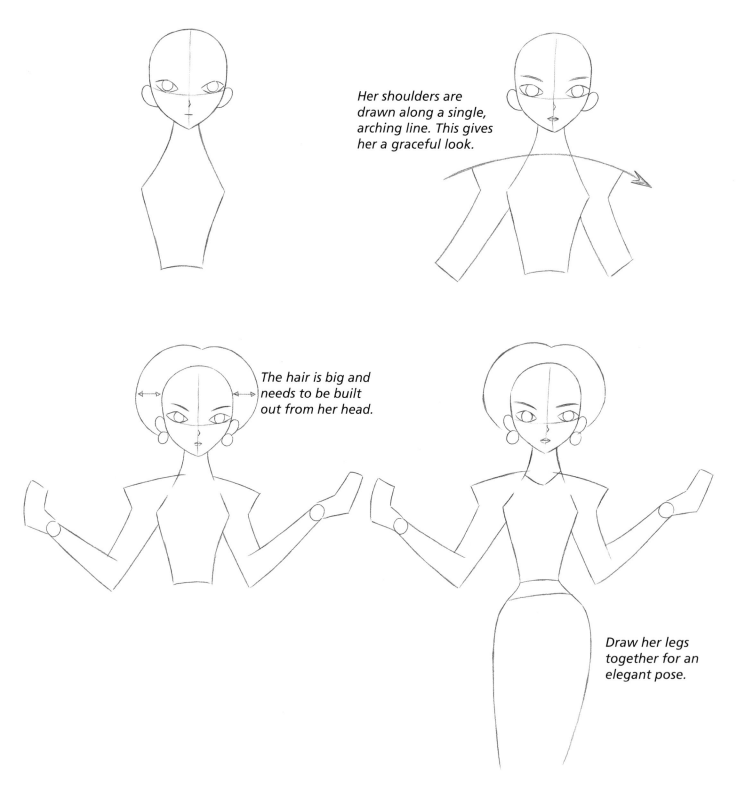

Her shoulders are drawn along a single, arching line. This gives her a graceful look.

The hair is big and needs to be built out from her head.

Draw her legs together for an elegant pose.

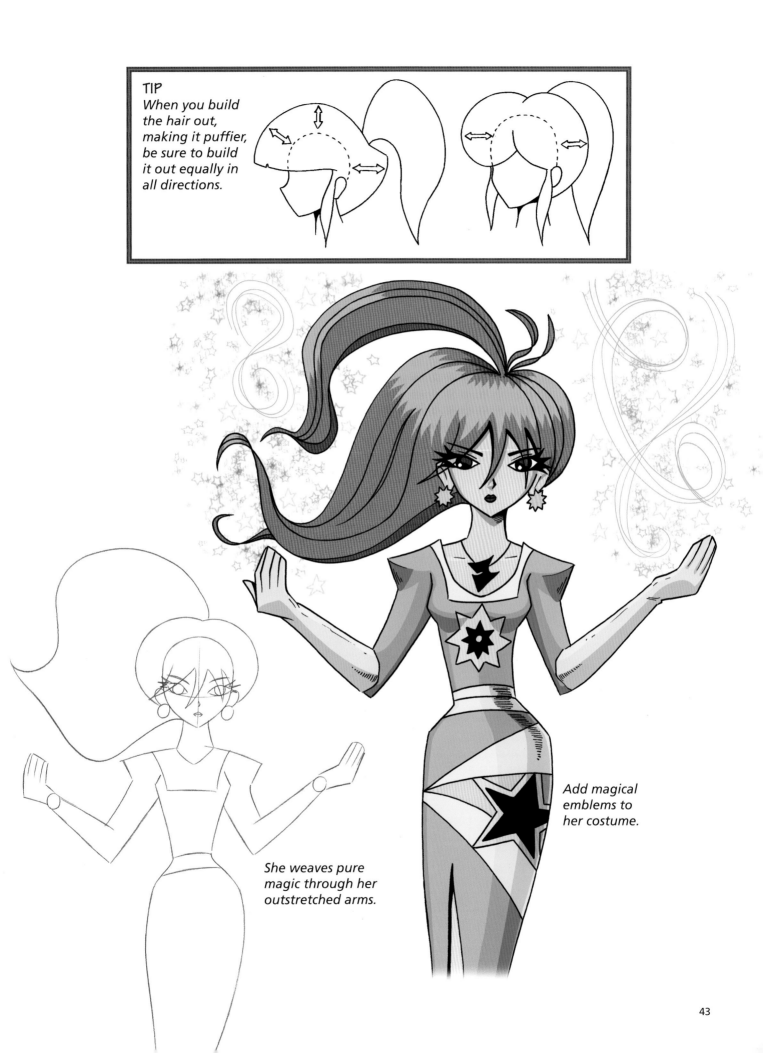

TIP
When you build the hair out, making it puffier, be sure to build it out equally in all directions.

She weaves pure magic through her outstretched arms.

Add magical emblems to her costume.

The Magical Staff

In fantasy manga, characters can summon great energies, and harness the forces of nature. With her tall magical staff this character is bringing forth a gigantic storm.

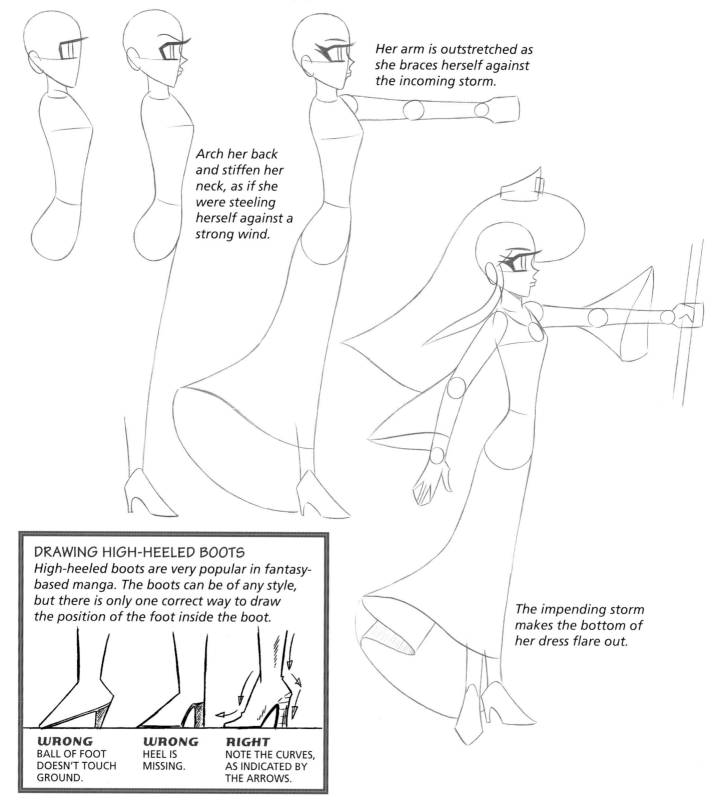

Her arm is outstretched as she braces herself against the incoming storm.

Arch her back and stiffen her neck, as if she were steeling herself against a strong wind.

The impending storm makes the bottom of her dress flare out.

DRAWING HIGH-HEELED BOOTS
High-heeled boots are very popular in fantasy-based manga. The boots can be of any style, but there is only one correct way to draw the position of the foot inside the boot.

WRONG
BALL OF FOOT DOESN'T TOUCH GROUND.

WRONG
HEEL IS MISSING.

RIGHT
NOTE THE CURVES, AS INDICATED BY THE ARROWS.

Magical Weapons

In the fantasy realm, weapons are spectacular and can summon massive amounts of energy from all directions. Although a dazzling weapon is eye-catching, to look brave, your character needs a heroic pose. The higher a knight holds his weapon the more fearless he will look.

WEAK

STRONG

HEROIC

HEAD TURNS

I'm reaching into the vault again. This technique is easy, but it will instantly turn an ordinary pose into a dramatic one. Most people draw the head facing in the same direction as the body. For a more dramatic pose, simply turn the head away from the body.

ONLY OKAY
The pose looks much weaker when his head is facing the same direction as his body.

BETTER!
This cool space guy's body is facing straight ahead, but he is glancing back over his shoulder. He needs to keep an eye on the alien invaders that are chasing him.

Power Packs

High-tech powerpacks are a cool addition to a whole bunch of characters. Don't be afraid to use futuristic equipment with medieval knights. The fantasy genre of manga is very versatile. Time periods are never kept pure. This adds more excitement to a story. There are many types of power packs.

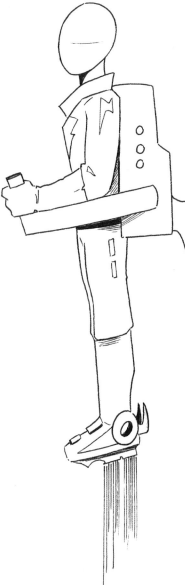

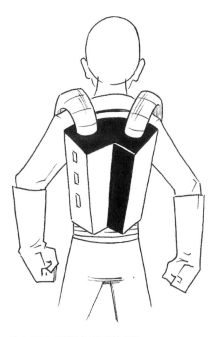

BASIC POWER PACK
This type is used as a reservoir of power, either to give the wearer extra strength or to power up the character's weapons system.

HANDS-FREE POWER PACK
The user can fly and use his arms with this jetpack. This is a great advantage for fight scenes in the air.

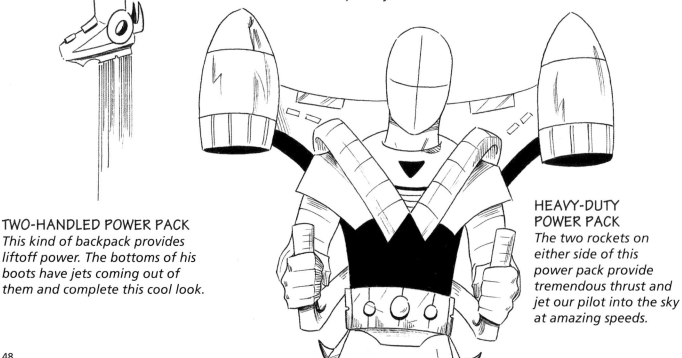

TWO-HANDLED POWER PACK
This kind of backpack provides liftoff power. The bottoms of his boots have jets coming out of them and complete this cool look.

HEAVY-DUTY POWER PACK
The two rockets on either side of this power pack provide tremendous thrust and jet our pilot into the sky at amazing speeds.

SUPERNATURAL BEINGS

The world of fantasy style manga is filled with imaginative and magical creatures that you won't find anywhere else!

Human-Animal Characters

Catgirls are popular in fantasy manga. These characters are a combination of humans and cats. The posture is totally human. But enough catlike traits are added to create a unique personality. Typically, cat ears, a cat's tail, and paws are added. Sometimes, whiskers and scruffy fur are added, too. But catgirls are always pretty characters, so be careful not to overdo the animal qualities.

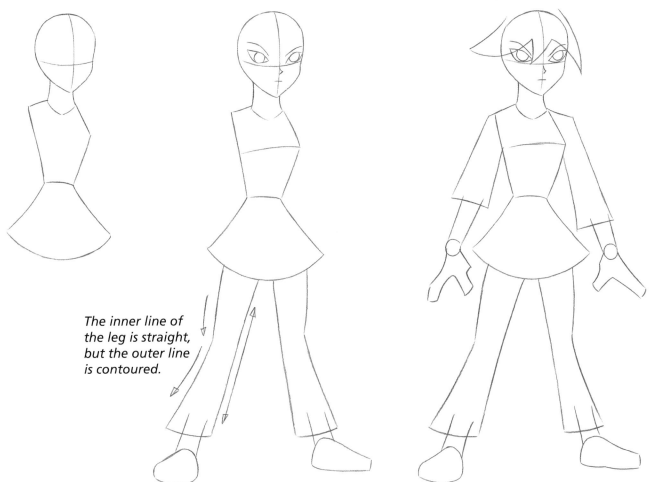

The inner line of the leg is straight, but the outer line is contoured.

A straight tail is awkward. Curl it for better results.

Wizards and Warlocks

Characters in long robes are easy to draw because most of their bodies are covered. The trick is to draw the shoulders extra wide; this will make your character look impressive. Most wizards have full beards and mustaches. They are also usually old, and a bit on the bony and creaky side.

HOW HIGH TO DRAW THE COLLAR
To make a character look more mysterious and powerful, draw a high collar.

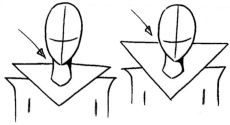

LOW COLLAR
looks weak
(collar at chin level)

HIGH COLLAR
looks powerful
(collar at ear level)

DRAWING WIZARD HANDS
Just like faces, hands have character, too. Make the hands bony for wizards. You can achieve this look by making all the fingers skinny, but bulging them out at the knuckles.

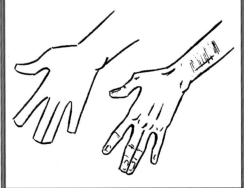

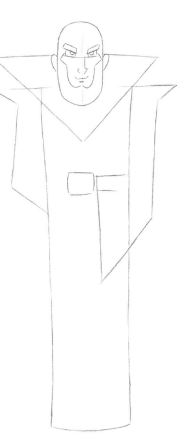

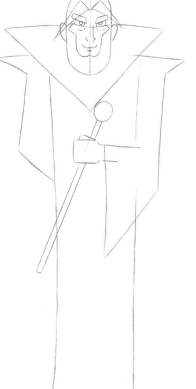

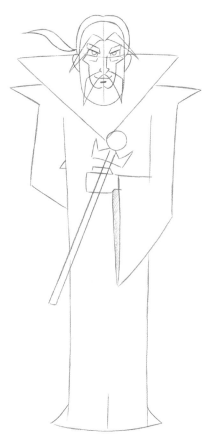

Mermaids of the Deep

These lovely creatures dwell in the sea. Mermaids have the head and body of a woman, but have a fish tail instead of legs. Let's take it step-by-step.

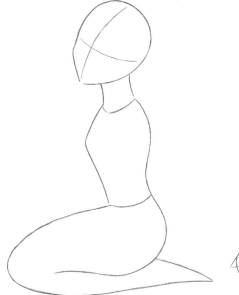

The line separating the human half from the fish half is drawn just below the waist. A slight uptilt of the head gives her a feminine look.

The shoulders add width to the upper body. She has elfin eyes and ears.

Draw two gently sloping lines from the neck to the shoulders. This is called the trapezius muscle. It prevents her shoulders from looking too square.

Remember to draw her tailfin flopping over, as indicated by the dotted line.

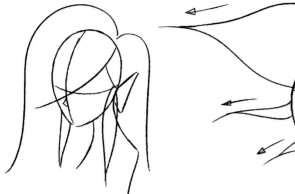

HAIR ABOVE GROUND—STATIC

HAIR BELOW THE SEA—FLOWING

DRAWING UNDERWATER HAIR

To make your character look as if she is underwater, make her hair respond to the ocean currents. This enhances her beauty. The hair should flow gently in one direction as if it were floating. Her hair should be huge, flowing, and beautiful.

Give her some kind of sea-oriented jewelry, like this necklace with a shell on it.

Demon Beast

This super-powered Prince of Darkness is an awesome figure. He should look harsh, with horns and spikes and battle-worn armor. The horns on demon beasts should always be giant-sized: no little "devil horns" for him! His long, draped outfit and shoulder flares let us know that he is the commander. The "V" at the top of his head is a common design in Japanese comics, and adds a cool look.

TYPES OF DEMON HORNS
Here are some other kinds of horns you can draw.

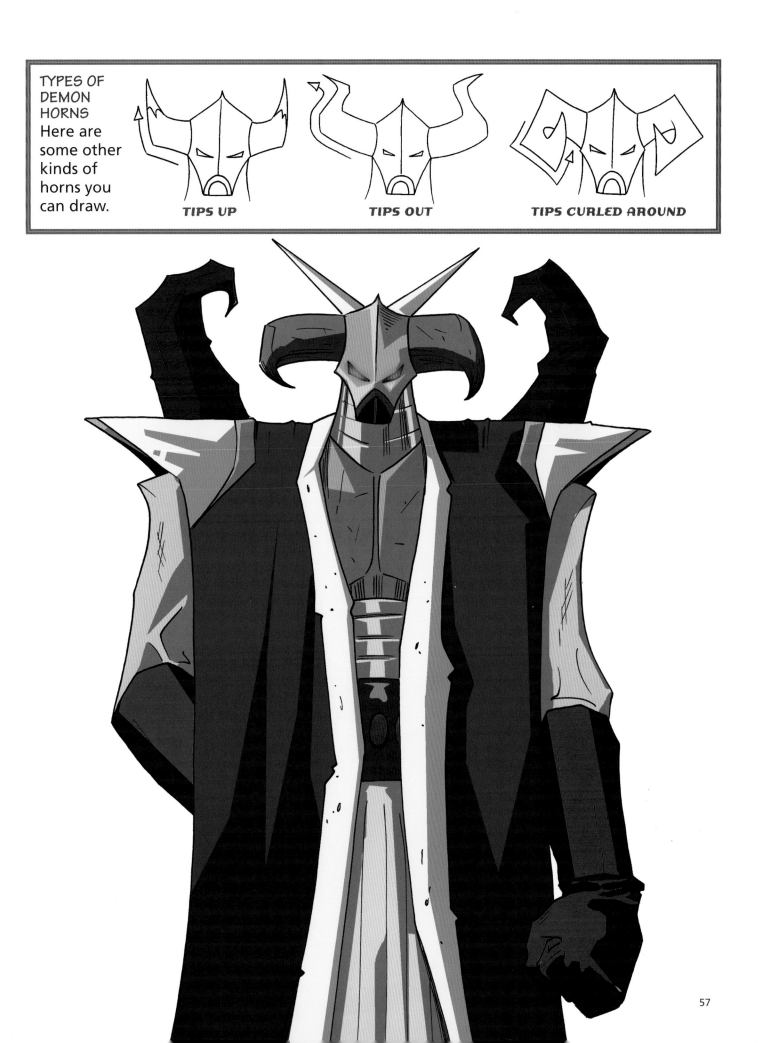

TIPS UP

TIPS OUT

TIPS CURLED AROUND

Mysterious Orb

Not all magical energy is good. Some is evil. Some even saps the strength of a character. This mysterious orb has been sent to find this girl and drain all of her life force. As it glows, it causes her to fall to her knees, which is a sign of weakness. A bent knee pose often conceals the rest of the leg and the foot as well.

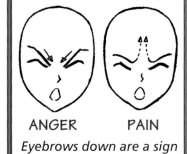

ANGER   PAIN

Eyebrows down are a sign of anger. Eyebrows that go down, but curve back up at the bridge of the nose, are a sign of pain.

PRINCIPLES OF PERSPECTIVE

Characters can look as if they are right up in your face or as if they are just a spot in the distance—it all depends on the perspective from which you choose to draw them. When drawing your character curve the horizontal lines (the ones that go from left to right) either up or down to get the right perspective.

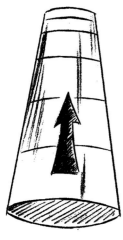

EXAMPLE ON A SIMPLE CYLINDER

We are looking UP at the cylinder above, therefore the horizontal lines must curve DOWN. Conversely, we are looking DOWN at the cylinder below, therefore the horizontal lines must curve UP.

When you want to make a character look really powerful, draw him as if he were standing over us and we were looking up at him. Draw him big at the bottom and narrower as you go up, and make all the horizontal lines curve down.

If you want to make a puny-looking character, draw him as if you were on the ceiling looking down at him. Draw him big on the top and narrower as you go down, and make all the horizontal lines curve up.

Awesome Character

With massive wings, bulging muscles, and wrists of steel, this awesome character is always ready for action. To make your character look really powerful, remember to use the principles of perspective. Draw him as if he were standing over us and we were looking up at him. Make him big at the bottom and narrower as you go up.

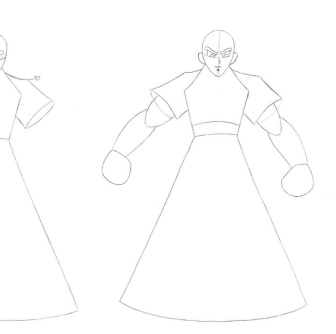

Index

The Challenge Drawing

This blazing, dramatic scene is an advanced drawing. However, I have broken it down into easy-to-follow steps. Ready to get started? Grab your pencil and saddle up!

CHARGING KNIGHT
Always draw the object a character is sitting on FIRST, before drawing the character. This principle is true whether the character is sitting on a throne, a jet-propelled motorcycle, or a horse.

The rider leans to one side so that he can swing his sword freely. (It also helps the picture, because he's not hidden behind the horse's head.)

The horse's chest intersects the neck about halfway up.

His upper legs go out to the knee, then angle down.

The horse's head fits entirely within the neck area.